what's real.

what's real.

poetry for everyone

ariv gupta

Edits: Hudson Billock and Ayushi Srivastava
Design: Anna Turysheva and Atharv Gupta
Funds: Shalini and Hitendra Gupta

Love you.

dedicated to
Mr. Thomas Seaton

to the first person
who gave me permission
to call myself a writer

i hope there is a library
up in the stars.

what's real?
many things
but also not many things
often it is hard to know what is
and what isn't

reality is up to the experiencer

what's real to you
may not be real to me
and what's real to me
may be preposterous to you

emphatically grand and painfully abstract
are the lines betwe   en the two

one moment may make sense of it all
the other may unravel everything
such is the life of a live-r

what's real has no predefined punctuation
capitalization
nor rhythm
except for a few exceptions
please place emphasis as you desire

what's real is what you want it to be

the following pages contain a
collection of such realities
strung together
in order of discovery
as life is

maybe reality is buried
beneath these pages

and though i may be blatantly lying to you
there is a magic to the realities traveled
and questions left unanswered

they sure do seem real to me
at least sometimes

within them
i hope there are strands of
real you find
and feelings you feel
that sharpen the lens
through which you experience
this moment

your moment

so here's an incomplete beginning
an attempt at piecing together existence
written in the form of feeling
by an all but perfect being

here's what's real.

realities

sol — 1

the desire — 3

back to feeling — 4

the in-betwe   en — 5

the lifelong learner — 6

nature's play — 7

here — 8

clap for me — 9

stability — 10

stasis — 11

the crack of dawn — 12

this isn't a real poem — 13

the source — 15

emotionless-fullness — 16

yosemite — 17

d i s t a n c e — 18

better than breath — 19

enlighten me — 20

to set an intention — 21

wheels on the bus — 22

the all nighter — 23

backlit — 24

freedom — 25

i said so — 26

acting 27

the year one thousand 28

silicon valley 29

you are 31

the key of life 33

genius 34

partly cloudy 35

surround sound 36

the better half 37

objective 38

19 39

me 41

if you get wet 42

based on my calculations 43

welcome to today 45

waiting for yesterday 47

your favorite loser 48

i feel it too 49

forehead split   ting 51

the way 52

how the world works 53

again 54

do or don't 55

your turn 59

read sparingly…

one reality at a time.

sol

a clock ticks, a bird chirps
a shriek pierces the air
in a cacophony of sensation
he begins to feel

his chest throbs
his veins pulse
blinking into existence
he twinkles in the light

a spark is his beginning
an ember in the sand
set on incubate
he searches for kindling

fixated on the answer
he grows frenetic
forgetting his inception
he scrambles for fuel

after exhausting every option
he returns to the spark itself
all his life he'd tried to create meaning
it's about time he let it find him

the soul transcends all
speaking out of turn
reminding us the search is eternal
it will never be done

so let go of the d
become one within
lean in to the me
and catch fire.

the desire

to mimic the majority
when the minority
are often better representatives
and reflections of a universal truth
while it may not be justifiable
they carry within them a certain sensibility
that with enough focus and discipline
anyone can master the human condition

to break away from the cyclical throes
of happy and sad, whole but still not swole
to remove the fleeting instances
that threaten a much greater collapse
than that of a casual saturday
without an intentional push to break free
one is left gasping, coughing, retching

a drug or a drink
life is much bigger than the kitchen sink
the minority knows this all the time
the majority finds out the sunday after
and after learning and then unlearning
unaware, unassuming, once again hidden
the key to freedom is left by its lonesome
for until next week it will remain
left to be desired.

back to feeling

college is a dreamscape
allowing you to be anything while tempting you
to remain the same
it makes you feel things
wrapping you in this moment
that moment
then the moment thereafter
and as you watch it all unfold you can't help but
wonder
what am i actually feeling right now?
college is special
curating month-like-weeks
and second-like-years
college ends before it happens

but home
home is a warm cozy blanket
that you refuse to get out from under
you hold onto home like a device with tiktok on it
unable to let go
as you remember those memories
relive those moments
as you fall in love again
home is the map lighting the path back to feeling
home lets you breathe
home is yours.

the in-betwe   en

emptiness
becomes
hopelessness
after mulling over it for a while

i miss having a persistent need to complete
an actionable task that fills the holes in my schedule
a purpose above the ego that affords me
the satisfaction of taking the hippocratic oath

the beginning is
as the zoomers say

slay

no one told me the in-betwe   en would lack
this naive energy

that "the journey" is cliche

as what's given is reclaimed
happiness becomes paid
and i go from intrigued to insane
a canonical phrase in my mind remains

a dead person would give their life to be in my
position.

the lifelong learner

a questioner of many
a learner of every
an explorer of the unknown
an aficionado of the known

a lover of the present
a worrier of making rent
both put-together and torn   apart
full of contradiction and peculiar-sounding fart

in this life-size body
sits a larger-than-life somebody
this monstrosity is a kid
a little naive, stew-pid

a far-fetched dreamer
a normal-seeking feeler
a hopeless romantic
a hope-filled fanatic

this purported lover of the above
every once in a while, needs a hug
a warm snuggle of their own
a reminder they're not alone.

nature's play

sweat speckled bodies
colored crimson red
the rolling sea matches the
footfall of pockmarked shoes

trees sway
the grass your favorite green
sunny bunnies
hop along the way

as they approach light speed
lavender blooms
cherries blossom
a familiar melody plays

the brush clears
the maze disappears
as the rhythm reveals
the oasis within

all our life
we search for ourselves
misplacing the key, forgetting
the door wasn't locked to begin with.

here

i have been given so much
yet know so little
truth can be so big
yet so brittle

what do i do? where do i go?
why can't i be an average joe?
who am i? who could i be?
why would the world ever choose me?

let go of knowing
let go needing an answer to keep you going
let go of the need for a perfect paragraph or phrase
let go of searching for an exit to this maze

the smallest moments, the greatest mirth
the answer is near
there is no justifying my place on earth
for i am already here.

clap for me

the confusion of past
a feeling-less pleasant
the uncertainty of future
the reality of present

now turns distant
a phrase is persistent
peace turns to pain
it's seventy degrees in vain

born with too much
i know too much
to be left to my devices
joyless vices

answer me please
am i alone in an eternal slumber?
must i wake up in disbelief?
i can't help but wonder

these moments of me
why must they be?
i need to believe
so heed my plea

clap for me!
let it be enough to be
clap for me!
my hands should be enough for me.

stability

if the ceiling has been met, it rises
if the floor has been found, it surprises
us with more to do
there's always something to do
to do, to do, to do
the mind is never at rest
it'll never be at its best
or will it?
will it?
who knows
so go
go go go
try this, try that
you're not a doormat
so move
move move move
why be you for another day?
go light the world on fire or something
stability is boring anyway.

stasis

everything is stuck
in color
out of color

in
the
betwe   en

immovable
rigid
firm

is our state
one that
getting out of

takes more
than a
bre|ak.

the crack of dawn

what about the untieable knot
what about the unmaintainable habit
what about those little thoughts
that run circles in your head like rabbits

the ideas that don't deserve
to be discounted at the dinner table
for being so fire they'd force an evacuation
of the latent sadness in the societal situation

those thoughts deserve a spot
on everyone's plate
like a special friend or the second date
it's never too late

to give in to the creative urge
and make it real
take it from mind
and meld to steel

and give it to those
it was thought up for
a small, but more
open door.

this isn't a real poem

i've spent a good portion of my life
thinking

thinking
about consciousness
reality
and the nature of being

and though i
believe i've come quite
f   ar
i can't help but recognize a
slowing down
of the epistemological epiphanies
i used to receive in copious amounts
all those years ago

i've reached a standstill
and it is as follows:

1. this is meaningful
2. i am meaningless
3. meaning is arbitrary
4. this is all temporary
5. i am my wallbreaker

i haven't got much more to say
in fact
like the pas…sage
of time
the numbers on the clock
haven't changed

there isn't a new way
to put this
or a way
at all

there isn't a number for 1:23
only a symbolic
tick on the clock

similarly i find myself full of symbols
in this case
feelings
and few syllables with which to express them
progress has screeched to a halt

the revelation that i am my undoing
but also my becoming
this is something i must meditate on

but what does this mean?

for meditation is all about
achieving presence in this moment
not a concept
nor an axiom

it is purely a sensation full of
rhythm
and
repetition
a song of sorts

i wonder what it sounds like.

the source

as i stare at the sky
i'm reminded of a
faraway night at nettle springs
where cicadas chirp and birds sing

the world is much brighter
a haven left by its lonesome
one finds solace in their company
becoming one with themselves

the campfire flickers
a chord is strummed
a voice cuts above the rest
on frequencies that yearn

how i wish to return here
away from the chatter of past and future
back to the present
a mainstay in the now
a pomodoro-less pleasant

but can't i create it here, now?
doesn't this sky run parallel
a universe alongside
the nettle swell?

the magic recedes
laying my eyes bare
as i return, motionless
to a dead-set stare.

emotionless-fullness

a mixture of nothing and everything
combined with both at the same time
a different type of crossed
this relentless animal
fades in and out
of the physiological sense space
beginning with detachment
followed by eyes bespeckled with water
the heart aches
the totality of self longs
for a far away feather touch
to numb and feel
to remember and forget
perhaps the shock the system needs
is the current

and yet

the morning's misery and yesterday's regret
make now that much more perfect
so let this moment fill thy lungs
in the belly goes that fresh scent
of all the colors of feeling and fret
a constant correct is nothing but cramped
so dive in headfirst
or walk in gingerly
let it rain, let it pour
let the ocean of emotion submerge you whole
for you are complete as you are
for you are enough as so.

yosemite

how does a gerbil know it's lunch time?
how does a bird decide to fly?
how does a boy know he's of age?
how does a parent know they must let him go?

aging is far from a numerical concept
it blurs the lines between internal and external
forcing fact and fiction to collide
how is it that one can feel one way
but have no choice but to obey the label given?

for eight and eighty can be felt concurrently
so let not numbers guide, but the universal me
life and death are but landmarks
what lies in between is a mystery

so walk, or clobber
up the steps of what was and what could be
it doesn't mind, why would it bother
yesterday or tomorrow, it's still yosemite.

d i s t a n c e

a forest of rock divides us
a long walk unites us
along we sing a song of silence
melodious as the cheery creek beside us

we traipse hand in hand
minds entwined as fingers
tracing the outlines of our past
in a circle of two

on our mouths words form
shapeless cuts from the deep
blood thicker than water, congealed
the breeze obfuscating the ache

bodies fuse together, carbon dating
turned to stone
a forest, created
out of our own harmony.

better than breath

there once was a day in a kitchen
that turned the mouth into a situation
you see, marshmallows were involved
indeed, sugar was what called

a hot fork to the tongue
was enough to get us rofl-ing
my brother laughed, i guffawed
my dad held his breath, in solidarity with my mom

now i'm laying on my belly
watching tv, making the rest of em jelly
for later that day i climbed a rock wall barefoot
and took a tumble, now i'm covered with soot

but it all sounds cooler than it felt
legend has it karma is still being dealt
for making my mom the butt of the joke
for it was i who swallowed the marshmallow whole

the score now set
my family gave me their best
or worst, depends on how you see it
i see it as love, you best believe it

because the light they share
makes the air that much more denser
why need oxygen in a sky so high
with people like these you could never die.

enlighten me

in a wilderness alcove
the eyes close
palms stretch outwards
focus is laid on the breath

a pulse appears
atop the forehead
a curious touch
a gentle nudge to focus on

straight from the source
energy emanates from within
in perfect harmony
with life's vibration

the body becomes symbiotic
with its surroundings
as the object of attention
makes its way through

golden light
pours out of the gateway
at once, home
in the body it never left.

to set an intention

today has begun
round two
and in its arrival
begets intention anew

will i be smart?
will i be strong?
will i be right?
will i be wrong?

yesterday was phenomenal
i could have died at its end
but it's time to attempt
the bonus level

because i get to do it
again and again and
you guessed it
again!!
so let's let life be the guide
because whether good or bad, it is
so let it flow
and let it go

entropy mandates it.

wheels on the bus

the vehicle parks
in a stark contrast from the beginning
i am left to carry my baggage alone
into territory far from unknown

panic grazes my chest

i walk into my new residence
new fragrances greet me
the walls are colored with history
written and unwritten

everything is everywhere all at once

a cacophony of chaos confronts the synapses
the city of stars turns sapien
the clock goes from analog to digital
the mountains turn to screensavers

where am i?
and why am i here?

part responsibility, part necessity
the reason is unknown
perhaps finding out
is why.

the all nighter
tired
eyes

whet
the sockets of time

for
their life span

is

      t
         i
            c
               k
                  i
                     n
                        g

          d
          o
          w
          n
          w
          a
          r
          d.

backlit

light is a silent emotion
why it allows us its embrace
i do not know
for its irreverence
rivals the deepest devotion
a constant companion
a lonely-not
light is yours
evermore.

freedom

the sheer luck
to be here
is a lottery
we win at birth

we cast it aside
call it normal
roll the dice once more
and tell ourselves

"i need it for tomorrow"

the birthday gift
has already been given
letting it take its course
is the celebration

so cash in your check
return to life's kingdom
as the mist clears away
take a whiff

ahh

it smells like freedom.

i said so

cancer
is fake
the carnal killer is as real as the ingredients
in a jamba juice shake

and then you find out your friend may have it
[insert bad word here]
stop it
this has to be a bit

but it's not

apparently
it's not in my hands

and apparently
no one's immune to it

and apparently
we don't get to decide how we die

apparently
cancer is real

what
the
hell

death isn't a fair teacher
life isn't any better
everybody dies
end of discussion.

acting

pretending to be someone else
all dolled up, waiting to break through
stepping into the other's shoes
wondering why it couldn't be you

flashing the high beams
we force undesirable parts of ourselves
to get out
of the way

to become a character
is routine
we do it
every day

but why shape shift?
why be different?
why play the bit?
am i not sufficient?

maybe acting itself
is an act of becoming
an emotional black belt
a well-deserved happy ending.

the year one thousand
bubble sort, mapping
natural language processing
the science of computing
is massively confusing

there's a limit to speed
everything shouldn't be rushed
so much is lost in translation
we don't need oral-b's new brush

the motors get faster
teeth fall off
the better chatgpt gets
the more we get laid off

slowdown is imminent
a world on pause
as the transition occurs
from digital to analog

your grandma will
be able to use the phone again
your mom will intercept your letters
to the old flame you nicknamed cayenne

but get this, it's fun
let's roll back the clock to y1k
because this time, when we rebuild
maybe this time we'll be okay.

silicon valley

novelty is finer than the most beautiful flower
a diamond in the rough
overused to the point of extinction
ingenuity is the currency of tomorrow

but payment is a feeble form of flattery
a sometimes weak excuse for attention
sometimes ingenuity is ingenuine
manufactured out of necessity

i often wonder how often
we create new things
not to do better for the world
but to help ourselves feel more meaningful

for applying adjectives
like faster, better, cooler, spicier
doesn't always result in improvement

a one-liner is cool
until it oversimplifies

personalization is transformative
until it's addicting

and medication is live-saving
until it's life-threatening

to be different
to get there first
to solve it before anyone else
to be your own hero

there's a reason viral and virus
both share the same word structure

with the beauty of the new
comes the terrors
of the unknown

sometimes old is gold
sometimes it isn't
there isn't a perfect balance with which to create
there is only coexistence.

you are
the ceilings
we walk under
and the walls
that enclose us
are constructs
we create
to make sense
of the universe

reality is terrifying
so we build explanations
to keep infinity at bay
till the next day
we are confronted
by the universal why

larger enclosures are built

the mirror fogs
till we forget it's a mirror
the walls close in
till they become home

inception occurs
self concept is born
necessity is created
should is pursued

too often is the search
for self discovery
conflated
with the discovery of self

at its core
there is nothing to prove

you are, period

you don't need an adjective
to satisfy
a craving for identity

nor a story
convincing your compatriots
of your usability

you are as special
as the trees
and the squirrel that climbs them

you are as beautiful
as the universe
and its sun-kissed horizon

so let yourself go
surrender to could
let should be

believe

and you shall be free.

the key of life

alone we are
yet so connected
detached personalities
yet so reflective
of a larger quest
a broader scope
than the point addressed

hollow metrics
dense spaces
emotional resonance
and pretty faces

average values
moonshot ideals
the human promise
is purely to feel

and what better medium
than your favorite
to lay down the foundation
of a lifetime of benefit

so pluck the keys
lay down a melody
the secret lies
beneath in the ecstasy

your story
in the key of life
now that sounds beautiful
to me.

genius

geniuses are made once a millennia
a perfect combination of mom and pop
a symbiotic state of perfection
a sunset made human

the genius embodies purity
finding order in disorder
our guide from chaos to clear
now or later, they're always here

the eternal constant
the indomitable spirit
that transcendent warmth
that imperfect perfection

yet the genius rarely travels
away from the incandescence
to gaze outside their window
bask in the magic they've made

open the blinds
take in the view
as the sun begins
to reflect off of you

because you are
the genius
get it
you.

partly cloudy

sadness clouds the soul
yet it's never felt clearer
the road to real gets steeper
yet it's never felt nearer

to be self sufficient
is like eternal crack
a replacement parent
a free pat on the back

but as the music crescendos
the heart restarts
self love isn't sufficient
but you could be.

surround sound

it's scary
when the music stops
the noise isn't canceled
the world cascades through your ears

within the torrential flow
one finds themselves in slipstream
with the creatures around them
slowly, falling in step with the rest

submerged, a breath is taken
simplicity overtakes skepticism
life flows down the waterfall
and sustains the swimmer

where were we before?
what were we before?
where are we headed?
do we need to go anywhere at all?

the head breaks through
resurfacing
ears clear
music returns

the world reappears
this time, distant
you were just here
weren't you.

the better half

gods creatures
longtime menaces
their starting line-up fills bleachers
as they sit with analysis paralysis

because, dang
we never measure up
to earn the coveted "i love you
-r best friend"

will we ever be enough?

why go on different dates
when we'd never get further
than best mate
at any rate

because to see, literally
to high five one time too many, physically
to hold them, even figuratively
is the prize itself, legitimately

life, liberty
and the pursuit of hot
what else equals happy
but the good old gyatt.

objective

beauty is all about perspective
a hint of a smile
scarily aggressive
a tip of the tongue
definitely oppressive

a bucket hat, a sunflower
converts the red delicious to cutie
a red flannel tee, a race across the street
gives the simp full knee mobility
sometimes willingly, sometimes begrudging
beauty is an everything smoothie

though it may be claimed opinion
beauty isn't always subjective
when the sun sets, and she's still glowing
the whole world stares, pensive
because for the first time
they too have a new objective.

19

it's weird to be nineteen
and okay at the same time
to let things pass
and not want to hold on
to welcome the cards life deals
rather than try and reshuffle
and wonder if you're lying?

its weird to be nineteen at all
and feel as though the age
of ninety is far better suited
for a mind as docile as yours

yet you're sharp
sharp enough to catch the figments of truth
embedded in the nighttime desperation
maybe it's easy to be okay
that's why you don't mind it

it's weird, though
because okay never felt this silent
this still
this quiet on the anthill
no this peace feels engineered
both organically and desperately
as if measuring its origin will help
keep the bridge from collapsing

its weird to toe the line
between independence and commitment
between hopefulness and trepidation
between yes and no

and to
in parallel
be unbothered
by the embodiment of either

it's weird to be human
and feel like an animal
to be a cold blooded creature
in a species of warmth

and yet the heat
won't permeate the inside
remaining a tomb
undiscovered
treasure unfound.

me

i overflow
as feeling fills me
to the brim and back

because i now remember
why i woke up today
in the first place

not for me
but for everybody
who made me, Me

the army of humans
who root for me
from every side of the line

life is
worth living
every second of

because to have a name
to be cared for
to have the luxury to complain

is worth every existential
crisis, every rejection
every tough conversation

because to have them
in the first place
now that is worth dying for.

if you get wet
you'll dry.

based on my calculations

the world is hard to believe in sometimes
that everything happens for a reason
when nineteen year olds get cancer
and chain-smoking ninety year olds get off scot-free

everyone should get to have kids

the math doesn't math up
when the nice guy loses
when she's deserved better
than bad company all her life

la la land should've had a happy ending

the calculator must be out of charge
when the character is praised
when they changed everyone's life
but still can't feel the joy of doing so on their own

the greats deserve to feel the part

and i'm definitely failing class
when the moment is so antithetical
when the happiest of places are experienced
through sad bodies and silent spaces

i need a break too

but in that tiny millisecond
when the heart palpates
when the feeling shoots
a superyacht's worth of everything down your spine

when the sun and the moon
hot and cold
and acceptance and rejection
become equally permissible

when it all starts to matter a little less
because it had never mattered
it simplifies to zero
or infinity

it's your calculation after all.

welcome to today

sighing, crying
fist folding, punch peppering
you've caused quite a mess
haven't you?

frowning, downing
upside drowning
sense isn't making
so i've got a rhyme for you

the fullness of flavor
a concurrence of crime
it's a freaky little thing
to be alive

so don't let the fickly feeble
undermine
the stupidly silly
and the sillily sublime

the crying and the quibbling
the figuring and wondering
why your friend's little brother
keeps calling you at the nighttime
(when your brother gave him your number)

to make thankless blunders
to dream and to wonder
to dislike happy and to like sad
depression is awkward, just a tad

because you see, my friend
we're all princes masquerading as paupers
hating life for putting us here
forgetting we are somebody's daughter

so allow rhyme to generalize
and fall under my trance
the luxury isn't in the best parts
but the worst ones at that

so dance, prance, be weird, be here
and bounce with me amongst the clouds
let hyperbole speak truth aloud
and start our adventure off with a bang

woah, hoo-hah, WOW, no way
let me be the first
my friend
to welcome you

to today.

waiting for yesterday

leaving me
on my own
my parents
headed out the home

teaching me, on
thanksgiving day
what it is like to be them
every day

waiting, hoping
that i'll come back
grace them with my presence
cut them some slack

for the daily act
of slogging and being
is punishment enough
for the price of believing

better is in the cards
tomorrow won't be today
as they ache in silence
waiting for yesterday.

your favorite loser

wrapped up in another's
held together in their arms
is a lot less majestic in the flesh

they've heard it's hot
sweaty
a mishmash of numb limbs

tangled
in a real life
t   w i s t   e r

though they wouldn't know
they've spent more time wondering than experiencing
specifically a one to zero ratio

but you might
yeah, You
they've had you on their mind all night

and they want private lessons
so come through
your favorite loser awaits you.

i feel it too

it's year two
with an onslaught of déjà vu
as we conduct them over and over
hellos, how-are-yous, and see-you-laters

i'm tired of being four feet away
from my best friend
and not being able to drive over
for fear of not spending enough time
with my in-house ride-or-dies

i'm tired of watching my childhood grow up
and not get the chance
to check in with it every so often
when facetime was literally invented to make it easier

i'm tired of watching my little brother get taller
and my mom and dad get older
while half of the time not being able to remember
my family is real

and i'm tired of about ten other things too
some because i'm actually tired of them
others because why not be tired further
when you're already running on fumes

they'll say stop crying, it's aight
now that's all bark and no bite
because for years they've tried
to wipe their memory fried

but the past is too fresh
it's ever-spesh
always a couple clicks closer
than the farthest hint of later

though the head is put on a swivel
and ms. congeniality becomes ms. split-personality
who says she's too far gone
it's never the right time to move on

anyways
see you in a couple days
okay, more than a couple
later's too long for me to say.

forehead split   ting

practical truths and
necessarily possibilities
unbelievable backdoors and
hopeless romances

this moment is far too transient
to squash all of the things into it
but that doesn't stop them from trying
to jigsaw themselves together

constant context switching with
evergreen embattlements
necessary numbness and
complete frazzlements

everything has changed
while in reality nothing has moved
but the car that inches forward
as physical and psychological drift

the forehead spl   its
the windows squeeze closer
the mountains spread wider
teasing an ejection of sorts.

the way

the gloved hand
reaches out of the compartment
where it was stowed away

wrapping around my larynx
it wages a war on my religion
the ability to explain it all away

saying placates the heart
etching out a personalized narrative
erasing the mind away

squeezing tighter
phrases that once made me sane
they burn away

the skin melts, the body crumbles
leaving, in its absence, the cowering soul
stripping it bare, taking ego away

because without the stories we tell
we are but wanderers seeking out reasons
wanderers, searching for a way.

how the world works

new shoes
sold to old fools
anything but gold news

cashews
diamond dudes
shampoo for soul food

upstream
in the inseams
hides the rockefeller dream

for it can't be earnt
against is the only current
green paper flows through

so get turnt, you've got some fishing to do
but hurry, catch something quick
before someone catches you.

again

my eyes glaze over
the world permeates within
a universe once hidden, found

again
my mouth opens
a smile tickles its corner
the heart remembers how to love

again
my legs ripple
suffused with pain and hurt
the body discovers its companion

again
my skin shivers
pura vida tickles the spine
reminding the self it still can feel

again
we breathe
doves in the wind

again
we breathe
in wordless ecstasy

again
we breathe
again.

do or don't

believe what you want
see what you feel
or don't agree with anything
i pretend to call real

you never had to listen to me
or anyone else
nothing is true
and everything melts

so while you're here
you might as well
go try something
ring up the almighty bell

there are many questions
to be solved
like how when i get older
i shouldn't have to be bald

but do keep me posted
that's the least you can do
when it comes to the answers
i haven't the foggiest clue

so do enjoy the ride
or don't
what's real is what you feel
just know you're not alone.

the end.

____

the beginning.

SO...

what's real?

your turn

59

the poet

ariv gupta inhabits the space
betwe   en the 8 and 80-year-old

he is a creator of music, poem, and art
a proud member of the anti-tech-tech-club
and, most recently, an ultra-endurance athlete

he is also a nationally awarded public speaker
and talented procurer of free time

he loves long windy conversations
laughable periods of confusion
and never having a plan

due to his eccentricity
some refer to him as "the brown dr. seuss"
others will tell you only he calls himself that

they are largely correct

he currently is a third year at ucla
and, as of this publication, single
find all things ariv at <u>arivgupta.com</u>.

9 798348 542375